VIENNA

Editions RISCH-LAU & GEBR. METZ Ges.m.b.H.

VIENNA FOR EVERYONE

Vienna is a town you ought to know.

Of every town you have certain expectations and images. Some associate with Vienna the waltz, delicious pastries, new-wine taverns, the Boys' Choir or the majestic Lipizzan stallions. For some, Vienna constitutes the metropolis of the Austro-Hungarian Monarchy that became a republic only by coincidence, and again others regard it as a junction between Eastern and Western Europe whose political and economic importance becomes evident every day. Whatever your expectations are, Vienna is waiting to be discovered. It is a town that demands a lot of its visitors if they intend to get a true impression. The detailed plan of the "Inner City" shows the

beautiful things to be seen. If they are mentioned in the text, it is easy to find them on the plan for they are all numbered. For lovers of Viennese cooking we have included, on pages 94 and 95, a number of the best known Austrian recipes. We hope that you will have an enjoyable and interesting stay, and we are certain that this Guide to Vienna will help you with its useful notes to get closer to this city and its

history. Because, like life there today, the spirit evolved from past epochs, and the people themselves, so the beauties of the city contribute to our understanding and appreciation of it.

A SURVEY OF VIENNA'S HISTORY

1st century
The Romans establish a military camp called "Vindobona". Celtic settlers are driven to the north. Next to the camp a civilian town is founded (relics have been found during excavation works). With the collaps of the Roman empire (5th century) the Romans withdraw.

10th century
Emperor Otto I establishes a border province of the Holy Roman Empire toward the east called "Ostarrichi", later "Österreich". It is ruled by the Babenbergs, who move their court to Vienna in 1155.

13th century
Vienna becomes a trade centre. Under the Babenberg Duke Leopold VI the city is extended with the fortification walls running along today's "Ringstrasse". In 1246, the last Babenberg dies.

14th century
1282: Beginning of the rule of the Habsburgs.
1365: Rudolf VI establishes the university of Vienna, the "Alma Mater Rudolfina".

15th century
At the beginning of the Humanism and Renaissance periods Vienna loses its economic importance. For 5 years it becomes the residence of the Hungarian King Matthias Corvinus.

16th century
1529: First Turkish siege to Vienna.

17th century
1645: During the Thirty Years' War, a Swedish army poses a serious threat to Vienna.
1679: The black plague ravages Vienna.
1683: Second Turkish siege to Vienna. A relief army of German and Polish troops help to release Vienna and force the Turks to beyond the Hungarian territory.
1717: Prince Eugene of Savoy defeats the Turks and Vienna regains importance.

18th century
Rule of Empress Maria Theresa. Supported by her advisers Kaunitz, Laudon, Haugwitz and van Swieten, she starts with important reforms such as the introduction of a new administrative structure, the land register, the successive numbering of houses and the first city maps. In 1754, the first census shows 175,000 Viennese inhabitants. She furthermore introduces compulsory elementary education. Her son Joseph II continues her work, guaranteeing the freedom of faith and religion through the "Patent of Tolerance", abolishing serfdom and monasteries not serving charitable and social purposes and reforming the health system. His opponents are of course numerous.

19th century
Napoleon besieges Vienna twice. After his defeat by England, Russia, Prussia and Austria the balance of powers is newly established at the Congress of Vienna, 1815. The leading personality at this congress is Duke Metternich.
1848: Liberal tendencies and revolutionary uprisings are suppressed. Emperor Francis Joseph succeeds to the throne as the ruler of the multi-national "Austro-Hungarian Empire".

20th century
1914: beginning of World War I. Emperor Francis Joseph dies after a reign of 68 years (1916). 1918: After the collapse of the Austro-Hungarian Empire the First Republic is established. 1919: First general elections for men and women. The Social Democrats gain the majority and start with a series of reforms such as th construction of municipal residential buildings. 193. Austria's forced integration into Nati-Germany make Vienna a province of the Third Reich. In 1944 aeri. bombardment of Vienna begins. In the battle for Vienr the Russian army forces the German troops to retrea After World War II Vienna is divided into 4 Allied occr pation sectors: Russian, American, British and Frenc. On May 15, 1955 the Austrian State Treaty is signed : Belvedere Palace. After the withdrawal of the occup. tion forces the Parliament on October 26 passes a la providing for Austria's permanent neutrality.

Vienna today
Inhabitants: 1.7 million.
Area: 157 square miles.
Altitude above sea level (centre): 547 feet.
Geographically, Vienna is situated at an air-line di

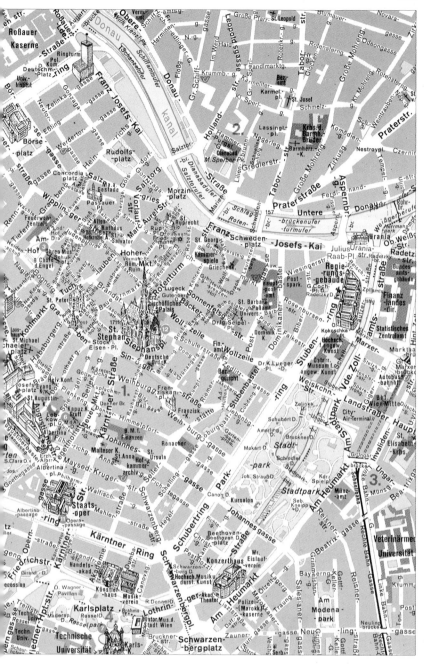

...ance of only 24 miles from the Czechoslovakian border and of only 38 miles from the Hungarian border. Vienna is the seat of many international companies and UN-organisations like the International Atomic Energy Agency (IAEA) and the United Nations Industrial Development Organisation (UNIDO). Due to Vienna's geographic position and Austria's neutrality Vienna has repeatedly been the venue of political summits (1961: meeting of Kennedy and Khrushchev; 1979: meeting of Brezhnev and Carter).

On January 1, 1995 Austria becomes member of the European Union.

The Viennese way of living

The stereotype idea of the Viennese charming, old-fashioned and polite, with fried chicken, roast pork, Wiener Schnitzel and pastries as their favourite dishes, with their love for Heuriger, music and art and their daily visit to their favourite café - is as correct as stereotypes can be.

Still, there is a core of truth in these partly ironic, partly sympathetic exaggerations: you do find the waiter at the café fixing the chair for the lady with a polite "Kuß' die Hand, gnädige Frau", the people singing at the Heuriger, the legendary pastries, the predilection for collecting dear (old) things and the people talking about good, old times. However, you will not find all this in places crowded with tourists but where the Viennese are among themselves.

Pedestrian precinct

Objects of interest (selection)

Stephansdom
(St. Stephen's Cathedral)

The construction works of Vienna's landmark lasted several centuries. In the 12th century a Romanesque parish church was built (outside today's city) and consecrated to St. Stephen. In 1263 the church was restored and partly rebuilt in the same style, in 1304 it was enlarged in Gothic style and in 1359 construction works of the nave (late Gothic) and the 137-metre high South Tower started. They were completed in 1433 under Rudolf IV (the "Founder"). The unfinished North Tower was capped with a Renaissance spire in 1579.

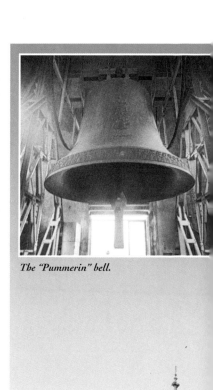

The "Pummerin" bell.

In the last days of World War II the church was heavily damaged by fire and all the Austrian federal states contributed to its reconstruction. Finally, a new bell, the "Boomer Bell" ("Pummerin") was suspended in the North Tower. It is rung only on very special occasions.

You can go up the North Tower by elevator and enjoy a marvellous view of the town.

From here you can see to the North the blue riband of the Danube running between the mountains of the Wienerwald (Leopoldsberg and Bisamberg), then to the South the panorama from the Kahlenberg to the mountains of the Anninger plateau, and, lastly, to the East, the wide Pannonian Plain with (if it is fine) the sparkling waters of the Neusiedler See.

Some of the outstanding parts of the church are: the Lady altar "Maria Pötsch", the high altar (lapidation of St. Stephen), the pulpit by Anton Pilgram (1515) chiseled out of 7 blocks of stone, the sepulchre of Emperor Frederick III in the right aisle (completed in 1913), in the left aisle the Altarpiece of Wiener Neustadt (Wiener Neustädter Altar) dating back to 1447 and the Tirana Chapel with the tomb of Prince Eugene of Savoy, the organ over the Giant Gate, the small 18th-century Baroque altars at the pillars, the ledgers and the memorial plaques at the side walls commemorating the people buried in the former church cemetery.

Next to the North Tower is the entrance to the catacombs, an underground burial place with the tomb of Duke Rudolf the Founder. Walking around the church you will find the funeral chapel where in 1791

the funeral service was held for Wolfgang Amadeus Mozart.

Next to the church coloured flag stones indicate the ground plan of the former church "Maria Magdalena" built in the 14th century and destroyed by fire in 1781. The Virgil Chapel (Virgilkapelle) situated exactly below the former church was excavated during the construction of the underground and can be seen from the station.

On the left page:
Wiener Neustädter Altar.
On this page:
Pulpit (above), High Altar (below).

Kärntnerstrasse

Karntnerstrasse joining the Stephansdom with the Opera, the most im portant and elegant shopping street in the city, is now a pedestrian zone. Several historic palaces (such as Palais Esterhazy and Palais Todesco) remind one of the historical importance of this stretch of street. Also noteworthy is the Malteserkirche (13th cent.) remodelled in Empire Style in 1808. Its Gothic interior houses pictures from the time of the cession of Malta to the British in the early nineteenth century, and also a marble monument to the Grand Master La Valetta who gallantly defended the Capital against the Turks in 1565.

Wiener Staatsoper
(State Opera House)

August von Siccardsburg and Eduard van der Nüll built the Court Opera House from 1861 to 1869 as the first monumental structure of the Ring Boulevard. After the widespread destruction of the interior by aerial bombardments it was reopened as late as 1955.

The Vienna State Opera is ranked as one of the world best opera houses. Among its directors were Gustav

Mahler, Richard Strauss, Clemens Krauss, Dr. Karl Böhm, Herbert von Karajan and Lorin Maazel. Its present director is Jan Holaender. Here, the famous Vienna Opera Ball takes place every year in the carnival season.

The orchestra of the State Opera is called the Vienna Philharmonic Orchestra and is famous all over the world. The State Opera's Ballet Company has also attained world renown through its tours.

It is possible to visit the Opera Theatre on days on which there are no rehearsals.

On the left page: Vienna Opera Ball.
On this page: State Opera House, ballet.

Maria Theresien-Denkmal
(Maria Theresa Memorial)

Designed by Carl Hasenauer it was made in 1874-88 by Kaspar von Zumbusch. The figures are in bronze. Maria Theresa was a very popular monarch, and many fundamental reforms were introduced during her reign, such as for example the simplification of the feudal state system, the abolition of torture, the introduction of compulsory schooling, the creation of a Civil Service, etc. The Universities were transferred from the Church and became State Institutions. Maria Theresa also managed to have 16 children during her

reign. Her son Francis Joseph II succeeded her on her death and continued, in the same spirit the reforms his mother had begun.

Museum of Fine Arts, inside.

Messepalast (Trade Fair Palace)
Behind the Maria Theresa memorial;
served as stables of the imperial
court. Designed by Fischer von
Erlach and built in 1723.

Naturhistorisches Museum
(Museum of Natural History)
Ended to be built in 1881. On display
are mineralogical, botanical, paleon-
tologic, zoological and prehistoric
exhibits.

Kunsthistorisches Museum
(Museum of Fine Arts)
To the left of the Maria Theresa memorial. Built by Gottfried Semper and
Carl Hasenauer from 1872 to 1891 in
the style of the Italian Renaissance.
Egyptian-Oriental collection, classi-
cal antiquity collection, collection of
coins and medals. Outstanding is the
collection of paintings by Dürer,
Rubens, Titian and Bruegel.
This imposing 4-storeyed building
has 2 internal courtyards and gives
prominence above the central block
to a large octagonal domed tower

Museum of Fine Arts

with 4 smaller open domes. Statues
and seated figures ornament the main
entrance to the building. An ample
vestibule and a well-proportioned
stairway welcome the visitor. Here
you will find works by Klimt,
Makart, and others.
Some of the collections belonging to
the Museum of the History of Art

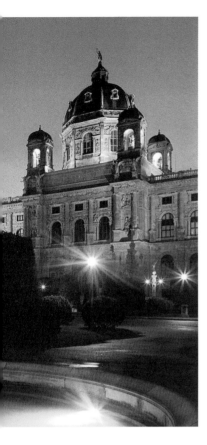

On both pages: some masterpieces from the collection of the Museum of Fine Arts.
On this page: Rembrandt's "Young Man Reading" (above); Rubens' "The Hildefonse Altar" (in the middle); "Self Portrait" by Rubens (below); "Madonna and Child" by Dürer (below).
On the left page: The Cellini "salt" (above); Bruegel's "The Dance of the Peasants" (below).

are housed outside the main building, as for example the collection of armour (Neue Burg), the Treasure of Sacred and Profane Art (Schweizertrakt der Burg), the New Gallery of Stallburg, and the collection of carriages for parades and for ordinary use at Schloss Schönbrunn.

Palais Prinz Eugen
(Palace of Prince Eugene of Savoy)

The Prince's Winter Palace is at Himmelspfortgasse No. 8. It was built between 1696 and 1724 by Fischer von Erlach and Lukas von Hildebrandt. The sumptuous rooms, including the Ball Room and the Entrance Hall, as well as the magnificent façade, are particularly notable. It is at present occupied by the Ministry of Finance.

Parlament (Parliament)

Designed by Theophil Hansen and built from 1874 to 1883 in the style of the Greek Revival. Until 1918 seat of the representatives of the Austrian half of the dual Austro-Hungarian Monarchy. Today, seat of the National Council and the Federal Council. In front: Athena fountain by the sculptor Karl Kundmann.

This two-storeyed building, constructed round some small internal courtyards, is very imposing with its four corner pavilions and raised wings. The main block, monumentally emphasized by the double ramped stairway with seated figures of philosophers and thinkers, is richly decorated.

The wings of the edifice have small central forebodies and atria. There are some lovely Corinthian columns on the ground floor to welcome visitors.

Palais Auersperg
Built in 1710 from designs by L. V. Hildebrandt. The central part was greatly modified later by J. C. Neupauer. Parts of the interior show influences from Classicism, while the rest is Baroque. This Palace and its garden are often used, because of their festive atmosphere, these days, by the organizers of balls and other events.

Rathaus (City Hall)

Designed by Friedrich Schmidt and built between 1872 and 1883. The wide Neogothic construction with certain elements in Renaissance style now houses the City Council Chamber, the Senate Meeting Chamber, the Red Hall, the People's Hall, the Mayor's Office, the Municipal Library, and the Archives of the City of Vienna. On top of the 295 foot-high central tower: the "Knight of City Hall" ("Eisener Rathausmann"), has become a symbol of Vienna. There is also a very fine carillon in the tower. During the Vienna Festival concerts are held in the arcaded courtyard.

The inauguration ceremony of the "Wiener Festwochen" (Viennese

Festival Week) traditionally takes place in the square in front of the Town Hall and is broadcast by radio and television.

In the park in front statues honour personalities like the composers of waltzes Strauss and Lanner, the Biedermeier painter Ferdinand Georg Waldmüller or Dr. Karl Renner, Federal President during the 1st and 2nd Republic.

Monument to Th. Körner, Vienna town Mayor from 1945 to 1951. President of Austria from 1951 to 1957.

The Town Hall around 1912. Watercolour by Franz Kopallik.

Universität (University)

Designed by Heinrich Ferstel and built from 1873 to 1883 in the style of the Italian Renaissance. Oldest university in German speaking Europe. The Arcaded Courtyard contains monuments to many outstanding scientists.

This complex includes one large quadrangle and eight small courtyards, while the main façade is characterized by projecting angular fore bodies.

The building of course can contain only a few institutions. The other faculties and institutes have been housed in new constructions in the neighbourhood or more distantly. Once a year, in summer, this famous edifice and its enchanting internal garden are the scene of the traditional University Ball. Facing its main entrance, across Ringstrasse is the monument (an obelisk 9 metres high) to Liebenberg, the well-loved Mayor of the town who distinguished himself during the Turkish siege in 1683.

Votivkirche (Votive Church)

Designed by Heinrich Ferstel and built in the style of the French Neo-Gothic cathedrals from 1856 to 1879 in commemoration of the unsuccessful attempt to assassinate Emperor Francis Joseph I (1853). As sponsor acted the later Emper or Maximilian of Mexico. Noteworthy is the "Antwerpen Altar" a masterpiece of Flemish woodcarving.

The square in front of this church is an important road junction (where tram, subway, and bus routes cross). Even if you are travelling by car it is possible to "change" here, for underneath the square is a large car park which is an ideal starting point for a tour of the city.

Maximilianplatz (now Rooseveltplatz) in 1906.
Picture by K.F. Gsur.

Rossauer Kaserne

This large brick building resembling a fortress was constructed in "Windsor" style after plans by Pihal and Markl (1865-69).

This architectonically imposing structure on the bank of the Donaukanal (Danube Channel) was built as an annexe to the Federal Administration Building (lower down behind the Urania), and contains stylistic elements modelled on it. (Finished in 1986).

In the small picture:
The Oktoneum, the new federal Building, built in 1986 by Architect Peter Czernin.

Schottenkirche and Schottenkloster (Church and Monastery of the Scots)

Between 1826 and 1832 Joseph Kornhäusl built a Neoclassical convent in place of a Gothic cloister, and replaced the outbuildings with a large three-storey apartment block. Inside the Convent the Hall, the Chapel of St. John, and the two storied Library with a barrel vault supported on columns are all interesting.

There is a picture gallery on the first floor, where you can admire, among other things, the 19 panels from the Gothic High Altar, by the so-called "Schottenmeister" (Master of the Scotsmen). Note also the interior of the Schottenkirche with an altar by H. Ferstl (1813).

The crypt is largely filled with tombs and is of great interest.

The Central Café in the Ferstl Palace.

On the left page: commemorative tablet to Liszt, Herrengasse 6 (above); view of the Schottenkirche (Church of the Scotsmen) around 1900, by Carl Wenzel Zajicek (1860-1923), below.

Burgtheater (National Theatre)

Designed by Gottfried Semper and Carl Hasenauer and built as Imperial Court Theatre between 1874 and 1888. After severe damages during the war reopened in 1955. It has held a leading position in the dramatic arts of German-speaking Europe. The decoration above the main doors shows "The Triumphal Entry of Bacchus and Ariadne", while allegorical representations of the Virtues and Passions which dominate Life and the Theatre appear on the side faces of the wings and on the back of the building. There are statues in the niches of the lateral façades. The stairs of the wings are embellished with works by Klimt and by Matsch. In front of the main entrance and the other side of the Ringstrasse is Town Hall Square, while on the right is the green area of the Municipal Gardens.

On the right page: Burgtheater, inside.

Volksgarten (Common Gardens)

Laid out in the place of the former Palace bastion; accessible to the public since 1823. Apart from the "Temple of Theseus" there are the monuments to Empress Elisabeth and to Franz Grillparzer.

Here Strauss and Lanner, followed by Edward Strauss and various other military bands, used to conduct their concerts. Nowadays the Gardens area includes an elegant café and an Open Air Dance Floor.

On this page: monument to Empress Elizabeth (below)
On the right page: Public Gardens, view of the Burgtheater (below).

Burgtor (Palace Gate)

This Gate was erected in 1821-24, with an order of Doric columns. It is decorated with Francis I's Latin motto: "Justice is the Foundation of Kingdoms".
In 1933-34 Rudolf Wondracek transformed it into a War Memorial for the dead of the 1st World War. After the 2nd World War there was also erected here a monument to those who fell in the Austrian War of Independence. There is a crypt beneath the monument.
The upper atrium, with no ceiling is decorated with artistic inlays of themes from the history of the Austro-Hungarian monarchy.

Neue Burg (below).

On the right page: monument to Archduke Charles (above left); monument to Prince Eugene (above right).

IVSTITIA. REGNORVM. FVNDAMENTVM.

Burggarten (Palace Gardens)

Formerly imperial gardens, accessible to the public since 1919; many memorials such as to Wolfgang Amadeus Mozart, Emperor Francis I (Franz Stephan of Lorraine, husband of Maria Theresa) and Emperor Francis Joseph. At the back side of the Imperial Gardens there is a palmery. The greenhouse, built by F. Ohmann, separates the Burggarten from the Albertina. Exotic plants can be admired here all the year round. The Burggarten is a favourite place for short strolls as it is a haven of peace and greenery only a short distance from the centre of the City.

Amalienburg and Leopoldinischer Trakt, headquarters of the President (above); Palmenhaus (below).

On the right page:
monument to W. A. Mozart (left), monument to J.W. Goethe (above right); monument to Emperor Francis Joseph I (below).

Neue Hofburg
(Residence of the Court)

To this most recent section of the Imperial Palace (construction works lasted from 1881 to 1913) an equivalent building on the opposite side (area of the Common Gardens) was planned but due to the disintegration of the Monarchy the project could not be carried out. It now houses the Ethnographic Museum (Museum für Völkerkunde), the Ephesus Museum, the Collection of Arms and the large reading hall of the National Library. The adjoining Congress Centre (the connection to the Leopold's Wing was built earlier) is the venue of numerous international conventions.

Neue Hofburg / Heldenplatz (Heroes' Square).
Monument to Prince Eugene.

The daily "Changing of the Guard" in the year 1912 in the Inner Court of the Castle. Watercolour by Franz Poledne.

Inside the Hofburg we must emphasize the Chamber of Sacred and Profane Treasure", at the entrance to the Schweizertrakt (The Swiss Wing). It holds the Imperial Crown of the Holy Roman Kingdom (about 962), the Austrian Imperial Crown with the Imperial Orb and Sceptre, the Treasure of the Burgundians, silverware, measuring instruments, ensigns, coins, medals, etc. Other parts of the Hofburg, such as the Amalienburg (Amalia Castle), the Leopoldinischer Trakt (the Leopold Wing), the Reichskanzleitrakt (the Imperial Chancellery Wing), the National-bibliothek (the National Library), the Spanische Hofreitschule (the Spanish Riding School) and the Great and Small Redoutensaal (the Hall of the Redoubts) etc., have been added in various building operations to the oldest part of the Hofburg, the Schweizertrakt (the Swiss Wing).

Emperor Francis Joseph I

Empress Elizabeth

The Imperial Crown of Austria

The Imperial Orb of Austria

Schweizerhof (Swiss Courtyard)

It is entered through the Swiss Gate (oldest part of the Imperial Palace; 13th century). From there, a pillared staircase leads up to the Treasures.

Across the yard there is the Imperial Court Chapel, where the Vienna Boys' Choir performs every Sunday, except in the summer.

The Spanish Riding School can be visited not only during the evening displays, but also on certain days of the week during "Morning Exercise". You must not miss seeing the famous white horses of the "Spanish Court Riding School of Vienna" showing of their proud action.

Schweizer Tor (Swiss Courtyard) above left.
The Spanish Riding School.

On the right page: the "Wiener Sängerknaben" (Young Choir), below.

Michaeler-Kirche
(Church of St. Michael)

This Church of St. Michael was first mentioned in 1267. The building was twice destroyed by fire (in 1267 and in 1327), the lower part of the octagonal tower was erected between 1340 and 1344. The Nikolauskapelle (Chapel of St. Nicholas) was added in 1350, the Dreifaltigkeitskapelle (Holy Trinity Chapel) in 1399, the Lukaskapelle (Chapel of St. Luke) in 1430, and the North Choir in 1476. A new tower with a spire was built in 1598. In 1626 the church passed to the Barnabites and a cloister and garth were added.

Michaelerplatz
(St. Michael's Square)

From here you enter the Imperial Palace through St. Michael's Gate (Michaelertor). To the right there are the state rooms with the Court Tableware and the Silver Depot. In the St. Michael's Wing were the private rooms of Emperor Francis Joseph I.

Michaeler-Kirche (Church of St. Michael).

Michaelertor (St. Michael's Gate), view of the church.

View of the Michaelerplatz, Michaelerkirche and Kohlmarkt; Watercolour by Friedrich Frank around 1910.

Michaelertor (St. Michael's Gate).

Josefsplatz (Joseph's Square)

From the architectural point of view one of Vienna's most beautiful squares with the memorial to Emperor Francis Joseph in its centre. To the right there are the Palffy Palace (1575) and the Pallavicini Palace (1784), to the left it is bounded by the building of the National Library designed by Fischer von Erlach and completed in 1737. More than 2 million books, documents and maps are kept here. The Grand Hall with frescoes by Daniel Gran dating from 1730 (in 1769 restored by Franz Anton Maulbertsch) is the most spectacular room. The Library wings with several ball rooms complete the building. From Josefsplatz you also enter the Spanish Riding School (Spanische Hofreitschule) another building by Fischer von Erlach. It is the world's largest winter riding school where riding performances are held and the famous Lipizzan stallions are trained every day. Across the street there are the Palace Stables (Stallburg).

On the right page:
Austrian National Library.

Albertina

The Albertina Collection of Graphic Arts in Augustinerstrasse was built by order of Duke Albert of Saxony-Teschen and completed in 1804. It comprises 230,000 works many of

Kapuzinerkirche / Kaisergruft (Capuchin Church/Imperial Burial Vault)

It is situated on the Neuer Markt and was consecrated in 1632. Under Emperor Joseph II the adjoining monastery was made smaller and partly transformed into a residential building. Below the church lies the Imperial Burial Vault (Kaisergruft). Only members of the Habsburg family were buried here since the early 17th century. To this day, the 138 coffins are guarded by Capuchin friars. If you join a guided tour you can admire the magnificent double casket for Maria Theresa and her husband, Emperor Francis Stephan of Lorraine, sculpted by B.F. Moll and in front of it - the simple copper coffin of Joseph II. Noteworthy is also the coffin of the Helvetian Henriette von Nassau-Weilburg who was the wife of Archduke Karl and the only non-catholic person buried here.

In the small picture: Kaisergruft.

which are permanently on view. It is the world's largest collection of graphic arts.

The Albertina Museum around 1910. F. Kopallik (below).

Graben (ditch) Column of the Plague.

On the right page: the Graben with the Plague Column around 1900. Watercolour by K.W. Zajicek. (above).

Graben (Ditch)

Once built to protect the Roman camp, in the 12th century filled up. When the town was enlarged for the third time buildings were erected here, too. Up to the 17th century, the square, surrounded by noble patrician houses, served as a market place. In 1679 the Trinity Column was erected by order of Emperor Leopold I as a sign of gratefulness when

the black plague subsided. At the time of Maria Theresa the square was the venue of numerous religious and Court festivities. Many of the old buildings were torn down in the 19th and 20th centuries.
Graben 10: Built in 1894 by the Art Nouveau architect Otto Wagner. Today it houses the studios of several famous artists.

Neuer Markt (New Market)

This second market square of ancient Vienna has a very eventful history. Around 1450 a pillory was erected here, in the 15th and 16th centuries it was the venue of tournaments and festivals and in 1708 Stranitzky, the "Harlequin of Vienna" (Wiener Hanswurst), had his stage of comedies on this square. During the war it was severly damaged but the "Providence Fountain" (Providentia), also called Donner Fountain (Donner Brunnen), was saved. The original statues were removed during the war and can be seen in the museum of the Lower Belvedere, the bronze copies date from 1873.

From the fountain you can see Plankengasse, at the end of which the City Church of the Swiss Protestants is prominent. Its façade is by Ignaz Sowinski (1887), though the church itself was built by Gottfried Nigelli in 1783-84.

Rafael Donner Fountain (left).

Petersplatz (St. Peter's Square)

Served as a market square after the removal of the church cemetery. Peterplatz no. 6: parish house dating from 1697.

Legend has it that St. Peter's Church (Peterskirche) was founded by Charlemagne. Great efforts to maintain the church made the physician, cartographer and historian Wolfgang Lazius in 1555 and in 1643 Franciska, Duchess of Palffy. The present building was begun in 1702 according to designs by Lukas von Hildebrandt and completed in 1733. Every Christmas there is a large crib exhibition. There are numerous works of art inside St. Peter's Church, including the fresco in the dome (the Assumption of the Virgin Mary, by M. Rottmayr), some paintings by Leopold Kupelwieser above the Tabernacle, the Altar Front by M. Altomonte, and the architecture of the High Altar by Galli-Bibiena.

This "Wiener Werkelmann" strumming for the crowd and satisfied with a few coins or the "Fiaker" are the last survivors of old-time Vienna. The "Fiakers" can be hired for attractive tours of the city. Their drivers are often expert guides to Vienna.

The "Werkelmann" (organ grinder).

Below, in the middle: Fiaker (carriage).

Below right: the new "Haas-Haus" built by the renown architect Hans Hollein (completed in 1990).

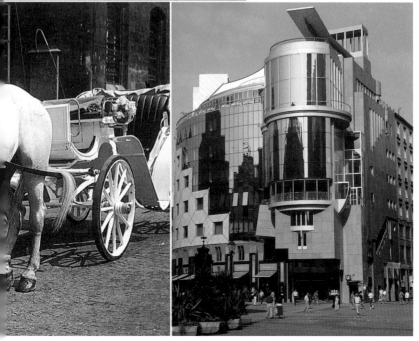

Platz am Hof (Court Square)

Here was the residence of the Babengerg Duke Heinrich Jasomirgott, built in 1155. In the centre of today's square: Our Lady's Column. The house Am Hof 7 (Märkleinsches Haus) was built between 1727 and 1730 according to designs by L. von Hildebrandt. Am Hof 8: 16th-century façade. Am Hof 10: Former Civic Armory built in the 16th century and remodeled later. It was with an assault against this armory that the revolution of 1848 started. Since the 19th century it has been the headquarters of Vienna's fire brigade also housing a Firefighting Museum. Am Hof 12: "St. Urban's House", dating from the 18th century. Am Hof 13: Collalto Palace, built in the 17th century. Here, W.A. Mozart had his first performance. The Church Am Hof (Kirche am Hof), once a Jesuit church, was built between 1386 and 1403 in the Gothic style. After a fire in the early 17th century the interior was adapted to the Baroque style, the Baroque façade was added in 1662. From here, Pope Pius IV, on his visit to Emperor Joseph II, blessed the people in 1782 and in 1806 it was announced from here that Franz II had abdicated as Emperor of the Holy Roman Empire of the German Nation. There is now a large underground carpark beneath the Am Hof Square, making it a very well known starting point for visitors to the City. Stephansdom Cathedral is only a few minutes away by foot across the Graben, and from there the most central part of the town is close by.

Judenplatz (Jewish Square)

Here were the Jewish school, the hospital, the rabbi's house, the synagogue and a bathhouse. Judenplatz 2: central part dating from the 15th century, Gothic relief shows the baptism of Christ. Judenplatz 11: Former Bohemian Court Chancellery, built by Fischer von Erlach between 1708 and 1714 and expanded from 1751 to 1754 by Mathias Gerl. Today: headquarters of the Constitutional and Administrative Courts.

The present synagogue is a few streets farther on in Seitenstettengasse. The monument in the Square of the Jews is to the poet Gotthold Ephraim Lessing, and recalls his work "Nathan der Weise" (Nathan the Wise) in which he argues for religious unity.

Monument to G.E. Lessing (above).
On the left page:
Kirche am Hof (Church of the Court).

Altes Rathaus (Old City Hall)

Wipplingerstrasse 8; replaced by the City Hall on the Ring in 1883. In the courtyard: "Andromeda Fountain" by Georg Raphael Donner, 1741. Today the house has a district museum and archives with documentations on Austria's fight for freedom.

The courtyard is particularly lovely as are also the reliefs on the ceiling of the Council Chamber and the Baroque façade with its imposing porch on Wipplingerstrasse.

Wipplingerstrasse leads out of the town over the "Hohe Brücke" (the High Bridge). Below it is the "Tiefer Graben" (the Deep Ditch) wherein there once ran streams and rivers, before the flow of the Danube was controlled. These water courses now reach the Danube underground. The cellars of houses adjoining it often have several floors.

Hohe Brücke and detail of the "Tiefer Graben".

Maria am Gestade
(St. Mary's Church on the Bank)

First documented in 1158. It was situated on a branch of the Danube River filled up later.

The Romanesque building was destroyed in 1262; its present appearance dates from the 14th and 15th centuries. The Gothic pierced spire is particularly remarkable.

This church has a troubled history. It was closed, as dangerous in 1786. During the French occupation it served as a military magazine, and then was reconsecrated and the redemptorists transformed it into a Czech National Church. Next to the Church there is a garage which offers easy access to the quay, and so to the centre of the town.

Hoher Markt (High Market)

Together with the Berghof, St. Rupert's church and the Kienmarkt, this square forms Vienna's oldest part. In the 14th and 15th centuries there were numerous guild halls and patrician houses and the municipal court with jail and pillory. In the basement of the house Hoher Markt 3 you can see excavations of Roman officers' houses, formerly situated along this "Via Principalis". Here was also the palace of the legates and the legion's headquarters.

The "Anker" Clock created by the painter Franz von Matsch is also worth seeing. The time is indicated by 12 historic figures (their names are written on a plaque at the house no. 12). At noon, all figures parade across the clockface.

The Joseph's Fountain (Josefsbrunnen) showing the wedding of Joseph and Mary (centre of the square) was built in 1732 by Joseph Emanuel, son of Fischer von Erlach, as a sign of gratefulness for the return of Emperor Leopold l's son from the Spanish War of Succession.

The "Hoher Markt" used to be a much favoured residential area in Old Vienna, and had some fine burghers' houses with rich decorations. But most of them were destroyed by fire in 1945.

Synagoge (Synagogue)

Built between 1825 and 1826 according to designs by Joseph Kornhäusl. Remarkable are the elliptical ground plan and the interior also by Kornhäusl. This synagogue at no. 4 Seitenstettengasse was the only one to escape burning on the "Night of the Glasses" in November 1938, and has been preserved till now.

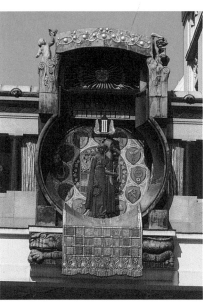

The "Anker" clock.

Ruprechtskirche (St. Rupert's Church)

Vienna's oldest church; founded around 740, Romanesque style with 2 Gothic annexes. In the interior you can well discern the different building periods. Interesting: The Altar-Piece of the High Altar is by J.M. Rottmayr (1708); the Gothic Holy Water Stoup is from 1500, the Organ Gallery with pierced railing is from 1439.

Postsparkassenamt
(Post Office Savings Bank)
Constructed by Otto Wagner between 1904 and 1906 in the matter-of-fact style of the Secession. The facing is in granite and marble, the fig-

The Greek Church

This church was built in the 19th century and completely remodelled in Byzantine style in 1858 after designs by Theophil Hansens.

The Church was popularly called "The Golden House", the façade is a rusticated construction in red and yellow brick, while the door jambs, the framing of the windows and the columns are of sandstone. All the ornamentation is in terracotta, gilded and set in a red and blue enamelled background. The pictures on the façade are by Carl Rahl, and those in the entrance by E. Bitterlich and August Eisenmenger.

Next to the church is the "Griechen Beisl", which is a restaurant with a peculiar frontage.

On the left page:
The Greek Church (above);
Griechen-Beisel (A typical Viennese
tavern), above right.

ures on the roof are of aluminium (O. Schimkovitz) and the interior (the Bank Hall) is also pervaded by a functional and sober style which is still almost modern.

Interior of the Post Office Savings Bank
(below).

Urania

The "Wiener Urania" is an "Institute of Popular Education" which was dedicated to lectures for popularizing science. It was built according to plans by Max Fabiani. Now it has a cinema auditorium and an astronomical observatory, which was reconstructed in 1957 after being destroyed during the war, and is now open to the public.

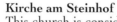

Kirche am Steinhof

This church is considered Otto Wagner's most monumental work. It was built in Art Nouveau style in 1904 as the church of the mental hospital. It stands on the highest point of the Gallitzinberg and is visible for a long way. Sculptures by Richard Luksch, angels by O. Schimkowitz, and glass mosaics by Kolo Moser decorate the building, which can be visited on certain occasions.

Prater

This traditional Viennese amusement park is highly popular in summer. Formerly the area was accessible only for the imperial family and was opened to the general public by Emperor Joseph II in 1766. Apart from the famous GIANT FERRIS WHEEL built by Walter Basset in 1896/97 there are many other attractions: the miniature railway "LILIPUT-BAHN", a 2.6-mile line going along all attractions of the Prater, the "LUSTHAUS", formerly starting point for hunting tours, today a restaurant (remodelled in 1782 by I. Canevale). The Planetarium (next to the Giant Ferris Wheel) with lectures featuring projections of the night sky given on weekends and holidays, and the Prater Museum displaying old pieces of popular entertainment.

Behind the Wurstelprater with all its attractions there extends the vast area of the Praterauen which provides those looking for exercise (cyclists, runners, horsemen) or sport with plenty of opportunity very close to the City.

This wide open space with its greenery and fresh air greatly appeals to the Viennese - in addition, naturally, to the restaurants and cafés - for Sunday walks.

The great chestnut avenues (for example the main avenue of the Prater) were planted by Ferdinand I (1537) and still provide most of the much-admired bloom on the trees of the Prater.

The Praterauen was a legendary refuge, also used by duellists who wanted to avoid being seen. The Prater was the site of a World Exhibition in 1897.

The world-famous Wiener Riesenrad (Giant Ferris Wheel).

Calafatty

Werkelmann

The LILIPUT train in the Prater (old locomotive)

Ice-cream seller

Lusthaus (Amusement House)

VIENNA INTERNATIONAL CENTRE

Completed in 1979 for the UN organisations already residing in Vienna: the International Atomic Energy Agency, the Relief Works Agency for Palestine Refugees, the Centre for Social Development and Humanitarian Affairs etc. The Vienna International Centre has extraterritorial status and was financed by the Republic of Austria and the City of Vienna. The symbolic yearly rent is 1 shilling. Guided tours are offered.

United Nations City is surrounded by spacious green partly because it is near the Danube, or rather the Donauinsel or the Old Danube. The large park was arranged in 1964 for an International Flower Show.

Orthodox Church.

Donauturm

Next to the Vienna International Centre are the 247-acre Danube Park (Donaupark) built on the occasion of the 1964 Vienna International Horticultural Exposition and the 827 foot high Danube Tower. By elevator you get to two panorama restaurants and the observation platform with an excellent view of the town and its surroundings (in beautiful weather even till the Hungarian border).

Islamic Centre

Hubertusdamm 17- 19.
The area is owned by 8 Islamic states, the mosk was financed by the former king of Saudi Arabia (Faisal Bin Abdul Aziz). It was completed in 1979 (the minaret is 105 feet high). A visit to the interior is possible.

Left: the "Donauturm".
On the right page: Islamic Centre.

Stadtpark (City Park)

Here, the Wien River is no longer roofed over. The stairs and walk ways on both sides of it were designed by the Art Nouveau architect Friedrich Ohmann.

At "Kursalon", a garden café, waltz concerts take place from Easter till late October. In the park, you find monuments to Johann Strauss, the "Waltz King". Here there is also Hübner's Kursalon, where in summer dances are organized to waltz music. These are rewarding social events immersed in an atmosphere of charm. The Public Gardens which cover the Glacis outside the city walls were planned by the landscape gardener Scellery and the town gardener Siebeck and are now practically in the centre, on the boundary between the 1st and the 3rd Bezirk, between the Grand Hotel Marriott, the Intercont and the Hilton. Their central position and their romantic layout make them a popular goal for tourists and for Viennese who want a stroll in the fresh air.

But the main attraction is the monument to Johann Strauss, the waltz king.

Hübner's Kursalon (below).
Underground Station "Stadtpark"
(public gardens).

Monument to Makart (above); monument to the "Waltz King" Johann Strauss (below).

*On the right page:
monument to Robert Stolz (above); monument to Franz Schubert (below).*

Palais Schwarzenberg

Built by Vienna's most outstanding Baroque architects, Lukas von Hildebrandt and Fischer von Erlach (completed in 1723). The complex is still privately owned by the Schwarzenberg dynasty, parts of it have been transformed into a hotel. In front of the palace is the "Hochstrahlbrunnen" (the High Jet Fountain) which was inaugurated in 1873 in the presence of the Emperor, on the occasion of the opening of the first acqueduct supplying Vienna with water from the Alps.

Hochstrahlbrunnen
(Fountain with high jets of water), above.

Hundertwasserhaus

A new and different Vienna. This house was built in 1986 following ideas and plans by the Viennese painter Friedenreich Hundertwasser, and is intended to be an example of individuality and a high quality of life as regards communal living, expressed in a new way. The eccentric, even bizarre, building has since become an attraction for lovers of the curious (Address: 1030, Löwengasse, on the corner of Kegelgasse).

House in which F. Hundertwasser lived (left).

Belvedere

Built between 1700 and 1725 summer residence for Prince Eugene of Savoy according to designs by Johann Lukas von Hildebrandt. The gardens were designed by the Bavarian horticultural engineer Dominique Girard. The building complex consists of the "Upper" and the "Lower" Belvedere and due to having been acquired by the Habsburg family houses important art collections. In the Upper Belvedere (Oberes Belvedere), which Prince Eugene used for representation purposes, is a gallery with works of the 19th and 20th centuries: Waldmüller, Klimt, Schiele, Kokoschka, Makart, Boeckl, Wotruba, Hausner, Lehmden and Hundertwasser. The Lower Belvedere (Unteres Belvedere), where the Prince used to live, houses a Baroque museum with works by Donner, Maulbertsch and Messerschmidt. In the orangery of the Lower Belvedere you find medieval Austrian works of art, Romanesque and Gothic wood carvings and altar pieces. Walking through the palace gardens you will have a wonderful view of the city of Vienna.

Upper Belvedere (above).
Lower Belvedere (below).

On the right page: wrought iron gate; interior of Upper Belvedere (below).

n 1945 both parts of the Belvedere were badly damaged, but it has been possible to restore them since, using the original drawings. In 1955 the Belvedere acquired an importance in international history, for it was in its Marble Hall, in fact, that the Peace Treaty was signed with the occupying Allies.

From that day Austria was free, and its political neutrality guaranteed.

Belvedere / internal view.

Karlskirche (Church of St. Charles)
Constructed from 1716 - 1737 by
Johann Bernhard Fischer v. Erlach
and his son Joseph Emanuel in ful-
fillment of a vow by Emperor Charles
VI during a plague epidemic in 1713.
It is Vienna's most significant example of Baroque sacred architecture
(the dome is 236 feet high).
The works of art by the sculptors
Mattielli and Stonetti, and by the
painters Gran, Rottmayr, and M.
Altomonte should be admired. The
angels on the steps are by Franz
Casper, the spiral reliefs on the
columns by Mader and represent
events in the life of St. Charles.

*Urban railway pavilion in "Jugendstil"
below.*

*On the right page:
Music Circle, inside / outside (below).*

Karlsplatz (St. Charles Square)

This square came into being due to the regulation of the Wien River (later roofed over) and the construction works along the Glacis (free area behind the city wall). Remarkable is the Art Nouveau "Stadtbahn Pavillon" by Otto Wagner. There is the University of Technology with the "Ressel Park" in front (named after Ressel, the inventor of the screw propeller) where you can admire the busts of 8 famous technicians.

Opposite is the "Musikverein" building designed by Theofil Hansen for the Society of the Friends of Music. From the large concert hall the Vienna Philharmonic's New Year's concert is annually transmitted to all over the world.

The building of the Music Circle also houses the Conservatory and vast collections referring to the history of music. They contain compositions, instruments, souvenirs, along with a library and music archives.

Secession

Built in 1897/98 by Joseph Olbrich as an exhibition centre for the newly founded association of avant-garde artists, "Secession". It was from here that according to the motto "To each age its art, to art its freedom" artistic innovations of the turn of the century emanated. On the occasion of the great Viennese Exhibition of Jugendstil (Youth Style) "Traum und Wirklichkeit" (Dream and Reality) in 1985 the Secession was also completely restored, and now again represents a particularly praiseworthy example of the style.

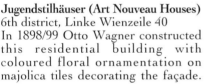

Jugendstilhäuser (Art Nouveau Houses)

6th district, Linke Wienzeile 40
In 1898/99 Otto Wagner constructed this residential building with coloured floral ornamentation on majolica tiles decorating the façade.

6th district, Linke Wienzeile 38
Also built by Otto Wagner with gilded medallions by Kolo Moser. These two houses form a beautiful and stylish background to the Flea Market.

Naschmarkt

This "Flea Market" offers every Saturday by-gones and real antiques from yesterday and the day before, mixed up with kitsch and worthless articles.

Those who really wish to buy something are advised to go early in the morning, for later everything interesting will have disappeared.

Schönbrunn Palace

Construction works started in 1696 according to designs by Fischer von Erlach. As the original plan to extend the "Gloriette" (Pavilion) to a palace proved too costly a "cheaper version" was built. In 1713, the palace was completed. Under Maria Theresa it was renovated and partly rebuilt.

Schönbrunn Palace was generally used as imperial summer residence and Maria Theresa lived here with her husband, Emperor Francis I, and her 16 children. It was in Schönbrunn that the 6-year-old Mozart was presented to the imperial family. During his campaigns Napoleon set up his quarters in Schönbrunn and his son from his marriage to Archduchess Maria Louise of Austria died here.

Emperor Francis Joseph I spent the last years of his life at this palace. 45 of the rooms are open to the public and are worth seeing. The splendid Rococo style of the rooms with a view of the beautiful palace gardens give a good impression of Austria's past. The gardens were designed by Jean

Trehet and later by Nicolas Jadot and were then redesigned by Franz Boos and Josef Riebeck. Noteworthy are also the Gloriette with the Neptun Fountain in front, the palmery, the zoo, the Imperial Coach Collection (with coaches, sleighs, sedan, chairs, ceremonial harnesses and liveries) and the Palace Theatre, which, after its restoration, offers performances every summer.

Of particular interest in the Park are the obelisk (Hohenberg, 1777), and the numerous statues - often hidden in niches in the trees. We recommend a pleasant walk after the essential tour of the Castle.

Schönbrunn Castle, at night (above).   *Pavilion (below).*

Schlosskapelle (chapel of the castle).

Nymphenbrunnen (above).   The Chambre of the Million (below right).
On the right page: Empress Maria Theresa, Emperor Francis I.

Tiergarten (Zoological Garden)

In 1752 the Zoological Garden of Schönbrunn was laid out on an interesting circular plan by order of Empress Maria Theresa. Lately, however, it has been greatly modified and reconstructed, and the enclosures have been adapted to modern concepts about the animals' requirements.

The "Palmenhaus" (Palm House) in front of the main entrance to the Zoo was built in 1882.
The Palm Court.

Grinzing

Grinzing is Vienna's most important vine-growing region where the famous "Heuriger" (this year's wine) is served. An Heurigen-tavern can be recognised by its bunch of pine twigs on the front of the house indicating that it is open. They may only sell wine from the own vineyard and have a buffet with warm and cold "Heurigen" meals. However, particularly in Grinzing there are also many restaurants. The genuine "Heuriger" with the "Schrammel"-musicians has become rare. Today, most of the places are without music.

Other Heurigen-villages on Vienna's outskirts are Heiligenstadt or Nußdorf, Sievering, Neustift, Salmannsdorf, Hernals and Ottakring and - to the south - Mauer, Perchtoldsdorf and Oberlaa. Across the Danube there are Stammersdorf, Strebersdorf and Jedlersdorf.

In Grinzing you can visit the parish church (Himmelstrasse 26) and the Beethoven houses in Grinzinger Strasse 64, Probus Gasse 6 (House of the Heiligenstadt Testament), Döblinger Hauptstrasse 92 (Eroica House) and Pfarrplatz 2. Beethoven used to move frequently so that there are 6 other Beethoven houses in Vienna.

Parish Church, Grinzing (above).
Beethoven's house, Grinzing (right).
Beethoven's house, Probusgasse 6 (below).

Kahlenberg

The church on the Kahlenberg dates from 1629. After severe damages it was rebuilt twice. Legend tells us that a mass was celebrated here in 1683 before the victorious battle against the Turks besieging Vienna. A chapel still commemorates the Polish King Johann Sobieski, the commander of the Polish relief army.

From the Kahlenberg you have an excellent view of the whole town and you should not miss going there especially in good weather. The "Höhenstrasse" - a fast road with access roads in each valley - goes south from Klosterneuburg through the Kahlenberg and the Wienerwaldberge, skirts the City and passes through the Wienerwald. This tract of woodland cannot be built on since it has been declared a protected green-belt zone, guaranteeing the town reserves of clean air blowing over from the West.

Kirche am Kahlenberg (Church).

Seegrotte

The "Seegrotte" (a lake cave) at Hinterbrühl, a locality to the south of the Wienerwald, 17 km from the centre of Vienna, is a fascinating tourist attraction. And in fact what one sees is something really sensational. In a gypsum mine, abandoned in 1972 because of the infiltration of water, in addition to the opportunity of admiring the old structure of the mine, one can sail on a subterranean lake - the largest in Europe (6200 m²). Furthermore, in the 2nd World War it concealed a factory making "Heinkel He 162" aeroplanes. It is open throughout the year and can be visited any day.

The natural miracle of the "Seegrotte" (above). Boat trip in the "Seegrotte" (Lake Cave), below.

Donauinsel (Danube Island)

Alongside the course of the Danube there has been set aside a huge 20 km tract, called the "Donauinsel" (Danube Island), dedicated to leisure time. All kinds of aquatic sports can be followed in their own separate areas - swimming, rowing, wind surfing, sailing, fishing. There is even an open-air arena and competition courses. In the middle there are extensive beaches, sports fields, barbecue zones, gardens and playgrounds for children, cafés etc. In winter most people there are ice skaters or langlauf skiers, while in summer the majority are cyclists. Altogether about 700 hectares (1730 acres) have been involved, including the areas of water, the dams and the islands; and the riverside meadows have been carefully integrated together with the established trees. This "island" is both restful and beautiful and the Viennese make very enthusiastic use of it.

The Weinviertel extends to the North of Vienna as far as the Czech frontier. As its name indicates this area is famous for its vineyards and above all for its white wine, lightly sharp and dry (Grüner Veltliner) which is very willingly drunk in the town, as is also Viennese local wine. The wine towns like Mistelbach, Poysdorf, and Falkenstein with their historical tradition of great wine making are favourite destinations for tourists, whose visits often end at a vintner's.

"Donauinsel", the leisure time paradise.

Klosterneuburg

Monastery of the Augustinian Canons, church dating from the 12th century, in the 17th century restored in Baroque style, two Neo-Gothic towers. Baroque interior; in St. Leopold's Chapel: remarkable altar by Nikolaus of Verdun dated 1181. In the monastery: treasury, library and imperial rooms.

The "Verduner" altar / Klosterneuburg.

Wachau Valley

A very beautiful section of the Danube valley with vineyards and fruit trees. Particularly during blossom time a preferred destination. Melk monastery: One of Europe's most important Baroque buildings, on a hill above the Danube valley, very interestmg from the architectural and artistic points of view, extensive library.

From Melk trip to Krems via Aggsbach, Spitz, Weissenkirchen and Dürnstein; great scenic beauty and many interesting places like castles and palaces.

The wine producing areas to the South of Vienna are also much loved by the Viennese. Walks in the Wiener Wald, cultural expeditions (there are plenty of castles and memorial places) and visits to the villages where the new wine ("Heurigen") is on sale are all part of this particular atmosphere.

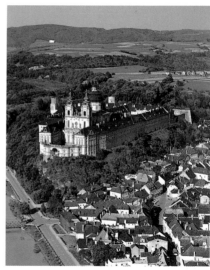

Stift Melk (Monastery).

Heiligenkreuz

Cistercian monastery with Romanesque church dating from the 12th or 13th century. In the cemetery: grave of Maria Vetsera who together with Prince Rudolf committed suicide at the hunting lodge Mayerling (at 22 miles) in 1899.

Petronell

Excavations of Carnuntum, the capital of the Roman province Pannonia (amphitheatre, Heathen's Gate, civilian town).

Stift Heiligenkreuz (Monastery).

Baden

Famous spa, known already by the Romans. Historical centre, park, casino, summer arena.

Lake Neusiedl

Europe's only steppe lake, 133 square miles, only 3 - 6 feet deep, very interesting from the scenic, climatic and biologic points of view. Through the southern part of the lake runs the Hungarian border. It is surrounded by famous wine-growing areas. Mörbisch, Rust, Neusiedl am See, Podersdorf and Illmitz are all situated at the lakeside and popular destinations for aquatic sports, wine tasting etc. Budapest, the Hungarian capital, situated within easy reach, also invites for a short visit. All destinations mentioned can ben reached by public transport, to some of them excursions are organised (travel agency or Sightseeing Tours). To Wachau-Valley and Budapest you can also go by boat.

Baden, Main Square.

Mayerling

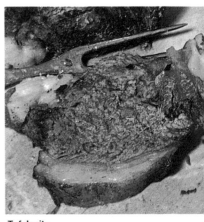

Leberknödel
Cut up 2-3 dry rolls and soak in water. Sieve finely with 100-200 g ox liver.
Fry chopped onion and chopped parsley in 30 g butter, then add to the liver together with a whole egg, salt, pepper, marjoram, 1 tablespoonful flour and 4 tablespoonfuls breadcrumbs. Mix well.
Allow to stand for 1/4 hour, then form small dumplings and simmer for 1/4 hour in clear meat soup.

Tafelspitz
Use a good quality piece of beef weighing 1 1/2 kg. Season with salt, pepper and finely chopped herbs. Place in a hot pan with 1/2 veal bones and brown on all sides to seal the juices. Add 1-2 tomatoes, 1 bay leaf, 2 cloves, lemon peel, peppercorns and 1/4 litre white wine. Add water, cover with a close fitting lid and cook until tender. Cut meat into slices and serve with fried potatoes, spinach (or leek sauce) and Apfelkren (grated horseradish and apple).

VIENNESE COOKING
Vienna's cuisine cannot be described as easily as that of other big cities. For it is characterised by variety originating from centuries of influences by the different peoples and cultures united under the monarchy. The culinary specialties range from Bohemian sweets to different versions of Hungarian gulash and to Serbian and Italian delicacies. The variety is continued in the restaurants: From noble places offering "La Haute Cuisine" to the typical "Beisl" with real Viennese dishes - you will certainly find what you are looking for. In order to give you a foretaste of the rich

Consommé with pancake strips
150 g flour, 2 eggs, 1/4 l milk, 50 g fat, salt.
Make a thin runny batter out of the flour, eggs, milk and salt.
Fry thin pancakes, roll them up and cut in strips. Add to the soup just before serving.

Milchrahmstrudel

Pastry as for Apfelstrudel.

Filling: Remove crusts from 6 rolls, cut up small and moisten in 1/8 l milk. Beat 4 eggwhites very stiff with 120 g sugar. Mix well together the 4 egg yolks, 60 g melted butter, 1/2 l cream, 2 tablespoons semolina, vanilla sugar, a pinch of salt and the moistened rolls. Then fold in the stiff eggwhites. Stretch the strudel pastry according to instructions, leaving broad strips bare around edge. Cover with filling. Strew 100 g raisins over this and sprinkle with melted butter. Roll up, place in fire-proof dish. Bake, covered, in hot oven for about 25 minutes. After about 12 minutes pour 1/4 l boiling milk, 100 g butter over strudel, return to oven and finish baking.

Viennese food we have looked up for you the recipes of some of the most famous Viennese dishes (taken from the book "Österreichs Küche", Rischbau in 6 languages: English, German, French, Spanish, Italian and Japanese).

Apfelstrudel

Strudel pastry: Work 250-300 g fine flour with 1 teaspoonful oil, a pinch of salt and lukewarm water to a softish paste until it rolls off the hands. Form into a ball, brush with oil and leave for at least 1/4 an hour under a warmed bowl. Roll out and then place on a cloth dusted with flour. Next pull the pastry out by hand evenly in all directions. Cut away the thick edge.

Filling: 1 kg ripe apples, 100 g butter, 100 g sultanas, 250 g sugar, 100 g breadcrumbs, cinnamon. Peel and core the apples, cut into thin slice and mix with sugar and cinnamon. Dot the pastry with butter. Fry the breadcrumbs golden brown in butter and scatter over the pastry.

Spread apple over approximately 2/3 of the pastry, and scatter sultanas on the top. Roll the strudel together with the help of the cloth so that the bare 1/3 is rolled in last. Place on a baking tray, brush well with butter and bake for 1/4 hour in a hot oven.

Sachertorte

Ingredients: 6 eggs, 160 g butter, 175 g chocolate, apricot jam, 160 g sugar, 160 g flour, 1 packet (2 tea spoonfuls) vanilla sugar, chocolate icing.

Beat the soft butter with half the sugar, the warmed chocolate and the egg yolks until fluffy. Whip the egg whites with the remaining sugar until stiff, add to the mixture. Stir in carefully the flour and vanilla sugar, previously seived together. Pour into cake tin and bake for an hour in a moderate oven. When cool cut in half, spread with apricot jam and sandwich together again. Also coat the sides and top with apricot jam, then cover thickly with chocolate icing. Icing: Warm 100 g chocolate carefully (not too hot). Heat 200 g sugar with water until it begins to stick together. Mix the lukewarm sugar with the softened chocolate and beat smoothly.

INDEX